JAPANESE ART
AND KOREAN ART

JAPANESE ART
AND KOREAN ART

General Editor
Francesco Abbate

English edition first published by Octopus Books
This edition published by Peerage Books
59 Grosvenor Street
London W1

Originally published in Italian by
Gruppo Editoriale Fabbri S.p.A.

ISBN 0 907408 27 3

Printed in Italy by Gruppo Editoriale Fabbri S.p.A.

CONTENTS

KOREA

The oldest works of art thus far discovered on Korean soil show an unmistakable Chinese influence. This indeed is hardly surprising, since Korea and China were bound together from the start of history. The story goes that Chi Tzu, a legendary figure, but regarded as the Korean people's first leader, was one of the Shang Chinese. However that may be, China had established a colony in Korea by 108 BC. It was located at Lo-lang, and many artefacts of Chinese origin have been unearthed from this site. The special importance of such finds lies in the influence they must then have exerted on local art. From the first century BC until the seventh century AD, Korea was ruled by three kingdoms – Koguryo (in the north), Paekche (in the southwest) and Silla (in the southeast). Eventually the kingdom of Silla absorbed the others, with military support from the T'ang emperors of China. It was known as the Great Silla kingdom and retained power till the tenth century AD. The first Koguryo capital was at T'ung Kou. Fine paintings from this period have been discovered on the stone walls of burial chambers there, showing an undoubtedly original touch. No more than traces are left of the Silla kingdom

1 *Korean art (Koguryō kingdom): Raised altar with Amitabha Buddha. AD 571. Coll. Tong-hyun Kim.*

Korean art (Paekche kingdom) : Plaque from Puyo. VII century AD. Seoul, rean National Museum.

1 Korean art (Koguryŏ kingdom): *Raised altar with Amitabha Buddha*. AD 571. Coll. Tong-hyun Kim.
Korean Buddhist sculpture was influenced by Chinese art; this piece reflects the style of Wei.

2 Korean art (Paekche kingdom): *Plaque from Puyo*. VII century AD. Seoul, Korean National Museum.
This terracotta plaque is a good example of Korean art documenting the Paekche kingdom.

3 Chinese art (Han era): *Gold and turquoise belt-buckle*. I–II century AD. Seoul, Korean National Museum.
This large buckle, found in Korea, is the finest Han specimen of goldsmith's work.

4 Korean art (Great Silla kingdom): *Plaque fragment*. VII century AD. Seoul, Korean National Museum.
Lokapāla is seated between two monsters; treatment of drapery and decorative detail shows rare skill.

5 Korean art (Silla kingdom): *Gilt bronze figure of Miroku or Bodhisattva Maitreya*. VII century AD. Seoul, Duksoo Palace Fine Arts Museum.
Influenced by Chinese models, it served in turn as model for the famous statue extant in the Kōryū-ji at Kyôto.

6 Korean art (Great Silla kingdom): *Urn*. VIII–IX century AD. Washington, Freer Gallery of Art.
Glazed stone-ware with an all-over geometric pattern, stamped and banded.

7 Korean art (Great Silla kingdom): *Wood statue of Yokasa Yurai*. VIII–IX century AD. Copenhagen, Danish National Museum.
Korean sculpture of the Great Silla period often looks archaic, like this statue of Yokasa Yurai.

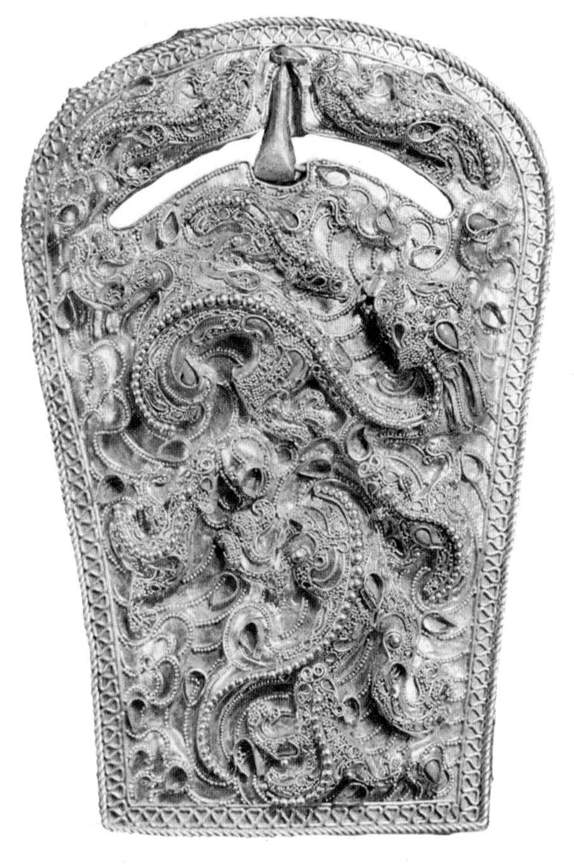

3 *Chinese art (Han era) : Gold and turquoise belt-buckle. I–II century AD. Seoul, Korean National Museum.*

4 *Korean art (Great Silla kingdom): Plaque fragment. VII century AD. Seoul, Korean National Museum.*

5 *Korean art (Silla kingdom): Gilt bronze figure of Miroku or Bodhisattva Maitreya. VII century AD. Seoul, Duksoo Palace Fine Arts Museum.*

6 *Korean art (Great Silla kingdom): Urn. VIII–IX century AD. Washington, Freer Gallery of Art.*

7 *Korean art (Great Silla kingdom) : Wood statue of Yokasa Yurai. VIII–IX century AD. Copenhagen, Danish National Museum.*

capital, Kyungju, but the few extant examples of ceramic ware are clearly modelled on contemporary Chinese products. The Paekche kingdom is far better documented. The Buddhist religion, which reached Japan by way of this kingdom, stimulated artistic activity on a broad front, particularly in the field of sculpture. The design of many Korean votive statues was assiduously copied by Japanese sculptors. During the Great Silla era, Korean artists tended to base their work on that of T'ang China, but were successful in retaining certain features from earlier days, which by that time had completely disappeared from the art of T'ang China.

From AD 918 to 1392, the Koryo dynasty ruled Korea. As happened under the Great Silla kingdom, centralized government again favoured patronage of the arts. The country enjoyed prosperity and security. Sculpture and lacquer-work, the latter especially influenced by China, both flourished, and ceramics too were of superior quality. Pottery, mostly in muted colours that ranged from green to grey, with black-and-white decoration, was much in demand. Forms were elegant and of sufficient linear appeal for the Chinese to find truly astonishing. A new technique, called *sanggam* (meaning 'inlay'), was not only most original but enabled Korean craftsmen to manufacture vases which looked every bit as splendid as Chinese lacquer-work set with precious metals.

Products using this technique have all the fineness of goldsmith's work. But inevitably there was a decline in standards. When the Mongols invaded, in AD 1231,

8 *Korean art (Koryo period) : Fragrance burner. First half XII century AD. Seoul, Duksoo Palace Fine Arts Museum.*

8 Korean art (Koryo period): *Fragrance burner*. First half XII century AD. Seoul, Duksoo Palace Fine Arts Museum.
Shaped like a flower of the lotus, and pierced. This technically-accomplished burner displays a manner as confident as it is original.

9 Korean art (Koryo period): *Ceramic dish*. XII century AD. Honolulu, Academy of Arts.
Inlay-work dates from the start of the twelfth century AD. Decoration on this ceramic ware was deeply incised, then coated in *barbotine* slip.

10 Korean art (Koryo period): *Ceramic vases*. XII – XIII century AD. Seoul, Duksoo Palace Fine Arts Museum and Coll. Hyung-pil Chun.
The vases are equally stylish in form; black-and-white *barbotine* inlay.

9

11 Korean art (Koryo period): *Ceramic pot of celadon type*. XII century AD. Honolulu, Academy of Arts. Loan coll. O.S. Picker.
In the twelfth century AD, Korean ware developed a local style, expressed in some fine celadons. Note the neat floral detail.

12 Korean art (Yi period): *White porcelain jar*. XVII–XVIII century AD. Ewha, Women's University Museum.
In the later years of the Yi dynasty, ceramics began to show some loss of quality. As usual in a period of decline, form tends to be top-heavy and the detail is less carefully applied.

13 Korean art (Koryo period): *Ceramic pot*. XI–XII century AD. Honolulu, Academy of Arts.
The decoration of this piece is well suited to the admirably rounded form.

10

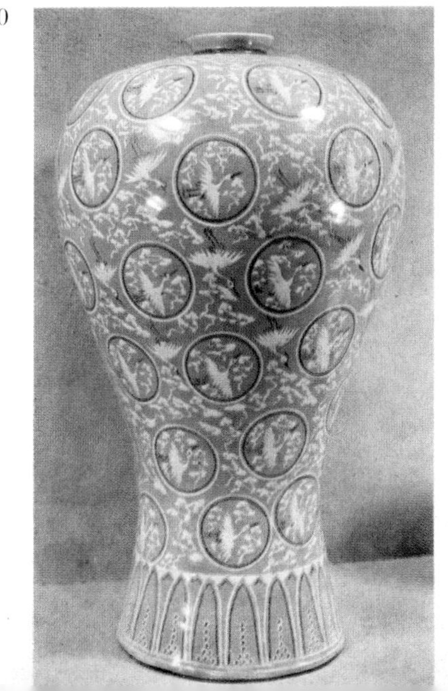

11 *Korean art (Koryo period) : Ceramic pot of celadon type. XII century AD. Honolulu, Academy of Arts.*

12 *Korean art (Yi period) : White porcelain jar. XVII–XVIII century AD. Ewha, Women's University Museum.*

13 *Korean art (Koryo period) : Ceramic pot. XI–XII century AD. Honolulu, Academy of Arts.*

the potters' studios of Korea were destroyed. A later attempt was made to revive the art, by copying earlier pieces, but the finished products were not anywhere of the same high quality. At the end of the fourteenth century the Yi dynasty succeeded the Koryo, and this house was to rule the Korean nation until the twentieth century (1910). It is a history of fluctuating fortunes, of victory and defeat, of war and civil strife, of decline and revival. Geographically placed between China and Japan, Korea was often a bloody battleground and frequently an innocent victim of events. Yet although invaded on numerous occasions and often devastated, Korea's extraordinary will and ability to survive ensured continuous, though irregular social and cultural development. Korean art, after the fourteenth century, was especially noteworthy for its ceramics and painting. The former was undeniably less elegant than Koryo work, but it had the virtues of being robust and utilitarian. As for the latter, it goes without saying that Chinese schools gave a lead to almost the whole range of Korean painting, both in choice of subject and in stylistic treatment. Nevertheless, certain artists showed outstanding talent and individuality; the work of Sin Yun-bok and Kim Hong-do, for example, depicted the natural beauties of their native countryside. Others followed Chinese models more closely, though often with a graceful individual touch added. Yi In-mun revived features from various ancient masters, in a style which was to prove popular in the Ming period. Chong Son, acknowledged as the finest and most invigorating landscape painter of his day, was influenced by the school of Wu; and Sim Sa-jong, also working under the pseudonym of Hyōnjae, produced delicate mountain landscapes clearly inspired by Chinese art, and ranks among the best of the scholar-painters. Yet Korean painting was also characterized by some very lively and fresh studies of animals, in all manner of attitudes. In these, as in many other representational works, despite obvious foreign influence, the Korean creative genius is seen at its best.

JAPAN

There is little factual information about the history of Japan prior to the year AD 552. In contrast to other great civilizations, this is a comparatively late date for recorded history to begin, and there is inevitably more than the usual amount of uncertainty and conjecture about preceding ages. The long period of Japanese prehistory is usually divided into two phases, known as Jōmon and Yayoi: the closing stage of the second one is called *Kofun* (the Great Tombs period). Jōmon culture lasted until about 200 BC. It represented a primitive society of nomad, food-gathering hunters, and unfortunately very little is known about this epoch. The only evidence consists of a few terracotta figurines of humans (probably idols) as well as some ceramic ware. The former belong to an early phase of social evolution when superstition was paramount, with universal belief in supernatural forces and free-play given to the imagination. Apart from the front parts, these figurines are roughly worked, and there

14 *Korean art (Yi period) : Portrait of a monk, painted on silk. XIV century AD. London, British Museum.*

14 Korean art (Yi period): *Portrait of a monk*, painted on silk. XIV century AD. London, British Museum.
Extant Korean paintings mainly date from the Yi era; they have affinities with Chinese Ming art.

15 Korean art (Yi period): *Tiger*, hanging scroll attributed to Sim Sa-jong. Seoul, Korean National Museum.
One of the best-known artists of the Yi era, Sim Sa-jong (1707–70) used the pseudonym Hyōnjae. A man of versatile talent, his traditional landscapes and animal studies are equally appealing.

16 Korean art (Yi period): *Landscape*, hanging scroll by Yi In-mun. Seoul, Duksoo Palace Fine Arts Museum.
Yi In-mun was one of the official painters attached to the art department of the court of Yi. His work is distinguished and he used a variety of pseudonyms.

17 Korean art (Yi period): *Water music*, album leaf signed Hyewōn. Coll. Hyung-pil Chun.
This delightful scene by the painter Sin Yun-bok, pseudonym Hyewōn, comes from a 30-page album which illustrates the charm of Korean life in the eighteenth century.

18 Korean art (Yi period): *Rocks in sea*, work signed Tanwōn. Coll. Hyung-pil Chun.
Hanging scroll, ink and light colour-wash, on paper. The few ink strokes and light colour effect bring this landscape alive. It is by Kim Hong-do, pseudonym Tanwōn.

19 Korean art (Yi period): *Landscape in rain*, hanging scroll signed Hyōnjae. Coll. Hyung-pil Chun.
Again, Sim Sa-jong shows his versatile touch in this landscape inspired by Chinese painting.

15 *Korean art (Yi period): Tiger, hanging scroll attributed to Sim Sa-jong. Seoul, Korean National Museum.*

16 *Korean art (Yi period) : Landscape, hanging scroll by Yi In-mun. Seoul, Duksoo Palace Fine Arts Museum.*

17 *Korean art (Yi period): Water music, album leaf signed Hyewōn. Coll. Hyung-pil Chun.*

18 *Korean art (Yi period) : Rocks in sea, work signed Tanwōn. Coll. Hyung-pil Chun.*

19 *Korean art (Yi period): Landscape in rain, hanging scroll signed Hyōnjae. Coll. Hyung-pil Chun.*

is no attempt to convey the three dimensions. Strange as they seem, they are not without mysterious appeal. The few examples of ceramics show a free-ranging spirit, but little conscious method either in respect of technique or decorative content.

In the second century BC, the middle prehistoric Jōmon culture was superseded by the later neolithic Yayoi culture (so named after a street in Tôkyô where the main finds were made in the year 1884), moving the power focus north of Kyūshū. Conflicting documentation has led some authorities to believe that this revolution was effected by an entirely different group of people, who invaded the Japanese islands and assumed control, driving out the earlier inhabitants. Others see Yayoi culture as a development of Jōmon. What is indisputable is that the Yayoi were no longer hunters, but farmers. Settled tenure of their land gave them the chance to take stock of their surroundings, for as their artefacts prove, they showed a keen appreciation of all forms of natural beauty. In shape and design, these have a child-like simplicity and freshness.

At the close of the third century AD, it became the custom to bury important persons in large funeral mounds; thus the period became known as that of the Great Tombs. It led to no startling innovations, but some of its fundamental features were to survive for many centuries in Japanese art. There was, however, some development of technique in the field of ceramics, if rather less flair than in the preceding Jōmon period. The most fascinating sign of the times was the

making of *haniwa*. These small figures, like *ming ch'i* in China, were usually laid in the grave to accompany the dead. Sometimes they represent humans or domestic animals, or dwellings. Unlike Jōmon figurines, they had no magical properties, but possessed a serene charm and innocent, poetic appeal. Japanese society at that time was organized in small communities, with powerful families occupying the position of overlords. One such family, from the fertile Yamoto plain, succeeded in unifying Japan, and in an attempt at conquest, established a permanent colony in Korea. These initial contacts with the Asian mainland gradually became more numerous and important, with far-reaching consequences for all aspects of Japanese art, society and civilization. In the early days, the Japanese learned to work bronze and iron according to Chinese style and technique. They made swords and buckles, bracelets and mirrors, and an object called *dōtaku*, the purpose of which is not known, but whose external decoration is the first example of genuinely Japanese painting.
Contacts with Korea were continuously maintained, but it was not until the year 538 that political and cultural links were officially confirmed. In that year an event of symbolic significance took place. From the Korean kingdom of Paekche, the Japanese emperor Kimmei was sent a great statue of the Buddha, in gilt bronze. In due course Buddhism, having reached Korea from the Chinese mainland and India beyond, became the official religion of Japan. From the outset the spiritual revolution encountered the opposition of

20 *Japanese art (Jōmon period): Figurines. Tôkyô, National Museum.*

21 *Japanese art (Jōmon period): Terracotta figurine. Tôkyô, National Museum.*

22 *Japanese art (Yayoi period): 'Haniwa' in form of monkey. Tôkyô, National Museum.*

23 *Japanese art (Yayoi period): 'Haniwa', martial figure. Tôkyô, National Museum.*

20 Japanese art (Jōmon period): *Figurines*. Tôkyô, National Museum.
Artists of the period tend to treat body form in rather summary fashion. There is a tendency to distort limbs and the effect achieved is one of heightened impact.

21 Japanese art (Jōmon period): *Terracotta figurine*. Tôkyô, National Museum.
The exact purpose of these terracotta figurines is not certain but may probably have ritual significance and possibly possess mysterious magical properties.

22 Japanese art (Yayoi period): *'Haniwa', in form of monkey*. Tôkyô, National Museum.
Modelling of form in the Yayoi period, by comparison with the preceding Jōmon period, is more skilful. The scheme is simple, linear treatment unemphatic. As a result, these figures have real 'body'.

23 Japanese art (Yayoi period): *'Haniwa', martial figure*. Tôkyô, National Museum.
This warrior in his protective armour was perhaps detailed for guard duty at the tomb where he was stationed. These small figures, like Chinese *ming ch'i*, are considered by some authorities to be substitutes for living victims, at one time sacrificed on the actual tombs.

24 Japanese art (Yayoi period): *'Haniwa'*. Tôkyô, National Museum.
In attitude and dress, similar to many *haniwa* figures, especially resembling them in facial expression. The wide eye-holes and the smaller slit for the mouth are rudimentary and traditional, not detracting in any way from the fine modelling of the whole. The lower parts of the figures terminate in a hollow cylindrical base, which was obviously intended to be inserted in the ground.

24 *Japanese art (Yayoi period): 'Haniwa'. Tôkyô, National Museum.*

vested interests, particularly the imperial guard, fearful of losing prestige and power. But the new faith made headway and was duly recognized throughout Japan. It stood for a higher quality of life than anything hitherto experienced, educating mind and spirit, and offering new horizons to human thought. In turn, the depiction of the deity in artistic terms was to inspire splendid work in many different fields. The first material effect of the new religion was in the building of temples, and the making of statues to place inside them. Models already existed in China and in Korea, but frequent warfare on the mainland was detrimental to the steady development of religious life and thought and many venerable works of art were destroyed. Japan was more fortunate. Here the Buddhist faith was uncontested and most of its art works preserved. Thus we have to go to Japan to study the best of Buddhist architecture and contemporary sculpture. The oldest Buddhist temple stands in the Nara district of Japan. It was built by order of the empress Suiko and her nephew and heir Shōtoku in thanks for the emperor Yōmei's recovery from a serious illness. This temple is called the Hōryū-ji, and remains the great showpiece of Asuka architecture. Temples usually lay on the inside of a walled precinct, with the main gate on the south. Within the precinct would be found the main pavilion (Kondō) and storied pagoda (exactly at right angles to the north-south axis), also the sleeping quarters of the priests or monks, together with their refectory and reading room. Most of the building was constructed of wood in the Hōryū-ji complex; the

25 *Japanese art (Asuka period) : Yakushi Nyorai or Buddha of medicine, attributed to Tori. VII century AD. Nara, Kondō of the Hōryū-ji.*

26 *Japanese art (Asuka period): Triad of Sākyamuni Buddha by Tori. AD 623. Nara, Hōryū-ji.*

25 Japanese art (Asuka period): *Yakushi Nyorai or Buddha of medicine*, attributed to Tori. VII century AD. Nara, Kondō of the Hōryū-ji.
In Japan, the introduction of Buddhism called for the building of temples and carving of cult statues. In due course a distinctively Japanese art form developed.

26 Japanese art (Asuka period): *Triad of the Sākyamuni Buddha* by Tori. AD 623. Nara, Hōryū-ji.
The Sākyamuni Buddha triad, in gilt bronze, is certainly the best-known work by the sculptor Tori.

27 Japanese art (Asuka period): *Kudara-Kannon.* VII century AD. Nara, Hōzō of the Hōryū-ji.
The figure of the goddess of mercy. The name 'Kudara' is a translation of the Korean 'Paekche' and has been said to indicate the statue's provenance.

28 Japanese art (Asuka period): *Komuku Ten.* VII century AD. Nara, Hōryū-ji.
Statue of a *Ten* or deity of the second order, a guardian spirit. The arrangement of drapery obeys a strict canon.

29 Japanese art (Asuka period): *Miroku.* VII century AD. Kyôto, Kōryū-ji.
This Miroku statue is like Korean work in style and arrangement. Some authorities tend to regard it as of Korean origin. The naturalistic face and stylized folds of garment are, however, specifically Japanese and of the last phase of the Asuka period.

30 Japanese art (Asuka period): *Kondō of the Hōryū-ji* at Nara. Early VII century AD.
Hōryū-ji was the first Buddhist temple in Japan, built to the order of the empress Suiko and her nephew Shōtoku. The Kondō is the main pavilion in the walled precinct.

27 *Japanese art (Asuka period): Kudara-Kannon. VII century AD. Hōzō of the Hōryū-ji.*

29 *Japanese art (Asuka period): Miroku. VII century AD. Kyôto, Kōryū-ji.*

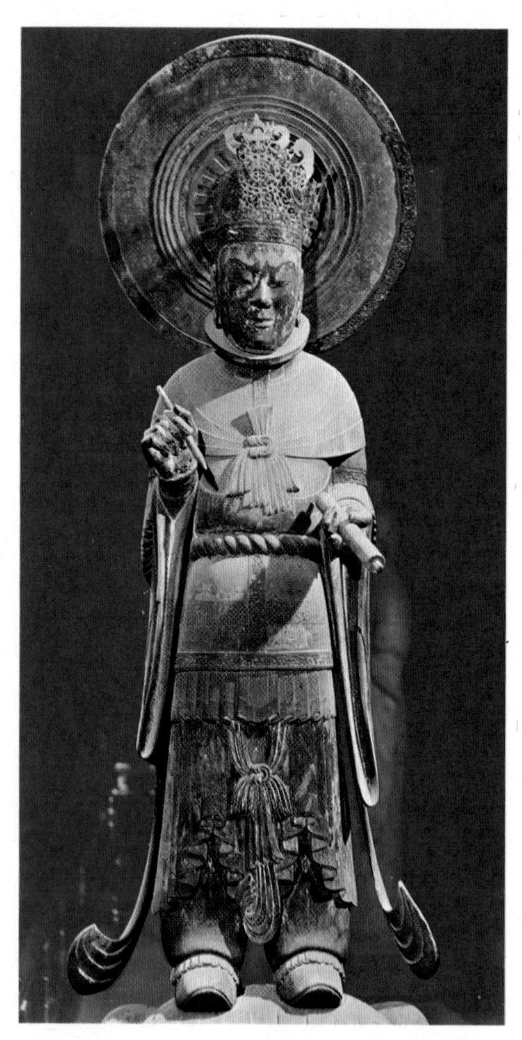

28 *Japanese art (Asuka period): Komuku Ten. VII century AD. Nara, Hōryū-ji.*

30 *Japanese art (Asuka period) : Kondō of the Hōryū-ji at Nara. Early VII century AD.*

above-mentioned main pavilion in Asuka style has fortunately been preserved.
Shōtoku is regarded as the real founder of Japanese Buddhism, and it was he who commissioned a great quantity of statuary for temple interiors. Among those to enjoy his patronage was the sculptor Tori who was responsible for the bronze triad of the Buddha between two attendants, in the Hōryū-ji. Tori's work shows a taste for balance, but stylized rather than naturalistic. Yet his human figures, with their long faces and rounded cheeks, are strangely impressive. The eyes are steady, the mouth half-smiling in the strange, enticing way of the ancient Greeks. In this Asuka period, another style, relying more directly on Chinese models, also found favour. Among the finer examples is the statue of Kudara-Kannon (or Avalokiteśvara), goddess of mercy. Here the body is better proportioned and altogether more lifelike, though there is still little effort at three-dimensional rendering. This style developed further, the line becoming simpler and more severe, the flow broken, a notable example being the Maitreya Buddha, housed in the Chūgū-ji.
Bronze and sometimes terracotta were both used for Japanese Buddhist sculpture, but examples in stone are rare, for this is scarce in islands of volcanic origin. Not surprisingly, the most common material was wood, a medium whose softness and pliability was preferred by Japanese sculptors. Asuka-style ceramics have not survived. Metal-work seems to have been of very high standard, especially in fashioning crowns and ornaments for the statues. Fabrics on

display in the Hōryū-ji, often embroidered, are proof of the advanced state of the textile industry in Japan at that date. Asuka-period sculpture was largely modelled on the style of the Northern Wei of China, though there was a time-lag. But in the early years of the seventh century, Shōtoku encouraged direct contacts with China. By this means, the splendours of T'ang civilization reached Japan, and affected all walks of life. In the year 645, the so-called Taila reform introduced the Chinese political system into Japan. Previously, there had been no proper Japanese capital. Now, such a centre was built at Fujiwara (south of Nara), after the style of Ch'ang-an, the fine capital of T'ang China. The years from 645 to 794 are known as the Nara period, and divided into two phases. During the first – Hakuhō (until the year 710) – the capital was at Fujiwara; in the second – Tempyō – the capital switched to Nara. T'ang civilization deeply influenced every form of Japanese artistic expression, though the results, especially in the provinces bordering China, were sometimes indifferent. Elsewhere, however, Chinese models were used with intelligence and restraint. Artists and craftsmen instinctively borrowed what was best in T'ang culture and civilization and Japan benefited accordingly. There were marked advances in sculpture. Gone was the stern approach of the Asuka period; the atmosphere was more relaxed and the general effect far more naturalistic. There was a boom in building. The eastern pagoda of the Yakushi-ji is an example; it was dedicated to the Buddha by the emperor Temmū, as a

31 *Japanese art (Asuka period) : Pagoda of the Hōryū-ji a Nara. Early VII century AD.*

32 *Japanese art (Asuka period-Nara period): Bodhisattva figure. Tôkyô, National Museum.*

33 *Japanese art (early Nara period) : Amida Nyorai with two attendant Bodhisattvas. Second half VII century AD. Tôkyô, National Museum.*

31 Japanese art (Asuka period): *Pagoda of the Hōryū-ji* at Nara. Early VII century AD.
The monastery is of exceptional interest for its beautiful buildings and harmonious setting.

32 Japanese art (Asuka period – Nara period): *Bodhisattva figure*. Tôkyô, National Museum.
This small statue is in the *hanka* pose, with the right leg crossed over the left, and the fingers of the supporting hand barely touching the chin. The flow of the garment and firmer body herald the new Nara style.

33 Japanese art (early Nara period): *Amida Nyorai with two attendant Bodhisattvas*. Second half of the VII century AD. Tôkyô, National Museum.
A bronze group which some authorities consider as the first evidence in Japan of the Amida cult, the Buddha of 'infinite virtues', always accompanied by attendants.

34 Japanese art (Nara period): *Triad of Amida*, raised altar in bronze. Early VIII century AD. Nara, Hōryū-ji.
Amida with his assistants is depicted against the background of a lake. The three figures rest on lotus flowers.

35 Japanese art (Nara period): *Yakushi Buddha*. Late VII or early VIII century AD. Nara, Kondō of the Yakushi-ji.
This is the central figure of the triad in the Yakushi temple. Dating is uncertain, some giving the year 697, others 728 when the Yakushi-ji was rebuilt at Nara.

36 Japanese art (Nara period): *Bodhisattva Gakkō*. AD 728. Nara, Kondō of the Yakushi-ji.
The Nara period has been described as the 'golden age' of Japanese art. Chinese influence predominated, lending Japan art forms and treatments, techniques and styles.

34 *Japanese art (Nara period) : Triad of Amida, raised altar in bronze. Early VIII century AD. Nara, Hōryū-ji.*

35 *Japanese art (Nara period) : Yakushi Buddha. Late VII or early VIII century AD. Nara, Kondō of the Yakushi-ji.*

36 *Japanese art (Nara period): Bodhisattva Gakkō. AD 728. Nara, Kondō of the Yakushi-ji.*

prayer for his wife's recovery. The Yakushi-ji represents a transitional style; Asuka elements are present but in addition there are two pagodas, instead of the traditional single one.

The change of capital from Fujiwara, too far south to function as a true political and economic centre, to Nara marks the beginning of a splendid period in the history of Japanese civilization. In terms of artistic activity, Buddhist sculpture and architecture still head the field. Glazed ceramics, after the style of T'ang China, are also noteworthy. Textile manufacture likewise reached a commendable standard, judging by the examples in the treasury of Shōsōin monastery, which have been preserved together with Chinese and Japanese furniture and household objects. There are some splendid examples of precious metalwork too, especially outstanding being the silver crowns for the statue of Fukū Kensaku Kannon, in a pavilion of the Tōdai-ji temple at Nara.

The Tōdai-ji, built about the middle of the eighth century, was planned on a large and complex scale. The two pagodas, originally planted outside the main courtyard area, were a new feature. Unfortunately, only the main building, or Hall of the Great Buddha, has survived. Despite restoration at various intervals, it remains an outstanding example of Buddhist architecture and the biggest wooden building in the world. The Tōshōdai-ji, a temple said to have been erected by the Chinese priest Chien-chên (Ganjin, in Japanese) who came to Japan to spread Buddhism, is also of real distinction. Other structures of the Nara

37 *Japanese art (Nara period) : Eastern pagoda of the Yakushi-ji at Nara. VII–VIII century AD.*

37 Japanese art (Nara period): *Eastern pagoda of the Yakushi-ji* at Nara. VII–VIII century AD.
The Yakushi-ji had two pagodas, of which only the eastern one remains. There are projections between storeys.

38 Japanese art (Nara period): *Fukū Kensaku Kannon*. VIII century AD. Nara, Hokke-dō of the Tōdai-ji.
A sense of grandeur emanates from this huge statue of Kannon, the Japanese counterpart of Kuan Yin.

39 Japanese art (Nara period): *Gigaku masks*. VIII century AD. Tôkyô, National Museum and Paris, Musée Guimet.
In the Nara era, a drama – the *Gigaku* – was popular and these wooden masks were worn by actors to hide the face.

40 Japanese art (Nara period): *Bodhisattva Nikkō*. VIII century AD. Nara, Hokke-dō of the Tōdai-ji.
Sculptures of the Nara era reflect a precise picture of art movements in China under the T'ang dynasty.

41 Japanese art (Nara period): *Tutelary deity Kongō Rikishi*. About mid-VIII century AD. Nara, Hokke-dō of the Tōdai-ji.
Figures of temple guardians were frequent from the late Nara period onwards.

42 Japanese art (Nara period): *Head of immortal warrior Meikire*. AD 729–66. Nara, Shinyakushi-ji.
Threatening of eye, hair standing on end, Meikira was intended to ward off potential temple desecrators.

43 Japanese art (Nara period): *Sage Furuna*. AD 734. Nara, Kōfuku-ji.
In addition to the eight guardians, the ten disciples of the Buddha are located in the Kōfuku-ji. Among them is the impressive figure of the sage Furuna.

38 Japanese art (Nara period) : Fukū Kensaku Kannon. VIII century AD. Nara, Hokke-dō of the Tōdai-ji.

39 *Japanese art (Nara period): Gigaku masks. VIII century AD. Tôkyô, National Museum and Paris, Musée Guimet.*

40 *Japanese art (Nara period): Bodhisattva Nikkō. VIII century AD. Nara, Hokke-dō of the Tōdai-ji.*

41 *Japanese art (Nara period) : Tutelary deity Kongō Rikishi. Mid-VIII century AD. Nara, Hokke-dō of the Tōdai-ji.*

42 *Japanese art (Nara period) : Head of immortal warrior Meikira. AD* **729–66**. *Nara, Shinyakushi-ji.*

43 *Japanese art (Nara period): Sage Furuna. AD 734. Nara, Kōfuku-ji.*

period lie in the Hōryū-ji complex, where they were put up in addition to the original buildings.
Sculpture of the late Nara period is on a par with the best work of the T'ang dynasty. Treatment of form is full-bodied, tending to naturalism, with perhaps a gentler touch than in the Chinese and original Indian models. The finest works include statues of the goddess Kannon: the Sho-Kannon, preserved in the Yakushi-ji, and the afore-mentioned Fukū Kensaku Kannon. In the Kōryu-ji, attractive statues of Miroku were inspired by the figure of Siddarta, the Sākyamuni Buddha to be. The statues of the terrifying guardians of the Buddha, placed around the deity, are strikingly lifelike; so is the portrait of the priest Ganjin as a blind old man whose attitude and expression conveys the power of the spiritual life.
During the reign of the emperor Kammu, in the year 794, the capital was again transferred, this time from Nara to Heian. It was an event of political and religious significance. Removing the seat of government from Nara meant a reduction of the excessive power which the Buddhist priesthood had gradually built up in that city. The running costs of all the monasteries, together with the tax exemption enjoyed by all religious orders, had been a burden on the national economy. With the move to Heian, the old monasteries suddenly lost influence. There was a new interest in mysticism, and two movements in particular, both of Buddhist origin, achieved widespread popularity. Known as Tendai and Shingon, they affected the climate of feeling and art in the Heian period. Both were religions

for initiates only, teaching the virtues of meditation and solitude, and disregard for everyday existence. Very soon new teaching monasteries were being built, not, on this occasion, in cities, but in the countryside, locked away among the mountains and in other inaccessible places. Because of the rugged nature of the terrain, these buildings differed radically from those of the Asuka and Nara periods, and were also far removed from Chinese models. If we are to judge from bronzes of the time, the traditional pagoda changed shape, the base being cylindrical, and topped by a raised and rounded roof. Further development in religious architecture came about through the cult of the Amida Buddha, which in turn called for more temples. The oldest of these, the Hōjō-ji, was destroyed, but some idea of their magnificence may be gathered from the Phoenix Hall of the Byōdō-ji at Uji near Kyôto. A rectangular pavilion, it has two wings terminating in small towers. Its light-bodied elegance is in perfect harmony with the underlying concept. Examples of dwelling houses have not survived, but are known to have comprised a rectangular centre unit, roofed and again often flanked by subsidiary buildings. The surroundings were invariably landscaped, with willows and cherry-trees. In the early years of the Heian period, sculpture kept to traditional lines, with wood used almost exclusively. Then sandalwood became fashionable (many series of statues were carved from this wood in T'ang China). The technique was comparatively rudimentary with the body carved from a single block.

44 *Japanese art (Nara period) : Yumedono or Hall of Dreams in the Hōryū-ji at Nara. AD 735–50.*

45 *Japanese art (Nara period) : Hokke-dō or Lotus Hall of the Tōdai-ji at Nara. AD 733.*

46 *Japanese art (Heian period) : Phoenix Hall of the Byōdō-in at Uji.*

47 *Japanese art (Heian period): Five-storied Pagoda of the Daigo-ji at Kyôto. AD 951.*

44 Japanese art (Nara period): *Yumedono or Hall of Dreams in the Hōryū-ji* at Nara. AD 735–50.
The many temples and shrines of this period are structurally akin to Chinese architecture of the same date.

45 Japanese art (Nara period): *Hokke-dō or Lotus Hall of the Tōdai-ji* at Nara. AD 733.
The Hokke-dō of the Tōdai-ji takes its name from a yearly festival called the Hokke-e which was held there.

46 Japanese art (Heian period): *Phoenix Hall of the Byōdō-in* at Uji.
The Phoenix Hall follows the style of palace residences of the period. It derives its name from the bronze phoenixes.

47 Japanese art (Heian period): *Five-storied Pagoda of the Daigo-ji* at Kyôto. AD 951.
Japanese love of formal elegance is here expressed, in one of its earliest masterpieces.

48 Japanese art (Heian period): *Bronze stūpa models.* Kyôto, Kurama-dera (left) and Nara, National Museum (right).
The typical form of stūpa (Buddhist shrines) may be appreciated in these bronze examples, made for sacred texts.

49 Japanese art (Heian period): *Wood statue of Shaka Nyorai.* mid-IX century AD. Nara, Kondō of the Murō-ji.
The colour tones which add a finishing touch to this statue underline its austere aspect.

50 Japanese art (Heian period): *Painted wood statue of Empress Shinko. c.* AD 890. Nara, Hōryū-ji.
Early Heian sculpture is marked by this very impressive style. The figure was carved about the year 890.

48 *Japanese art (Heian period) : Bronze stūpa models. Kyôto, Kurama-dera (on the left) and Nara, National Museum (on the right).*

49 *Japanese art (Heian period) : Wood statue of Shaka Nyorai. Mid-IX century AD. Nara, Kondō of the Murō-ji.*

50 *Japanese art (Heian period) : Painted wood statue of empress Shinko. c. AD 890. Nara, Hōryū-ji.*

Buddhas of the period are corpulent and severe of aspect, yet not without an awesome majesty. At the same time, there was a Shinto revival. This ancient Japanese religion had been driven underground by Buddhism. But now it re-emerged, subtly commingled with Buddhist doctrine. This provided sculptors with new subjects, such as the goddess Nakatsu-hime – vigorously represented in polychrome wood.

In the tenth century, great changes occurred in the fabric of Japanese society and these in turn affected the figurative arts. The fall of the T'ang dynasty in China was followed by civil unrest and the breakdown of government. The long-standing social and artistic links between the two countries were progressively weakened. A new religious movement in Japan, dedicated to the Amida Buddha, then secured a large following. In court circles, power was concentrated in the hands of noble families, who monopolized the higher state offices. One family in particular, the Fujiwara, was so powerful that the Heian period from the tenth century is also referred to as Fujiwara. Once again, there was a revival of temple and monastery building, and eminent sculptors were commissioned to produce appropriate work for the interiors.

The most celebrated of these sculptors was Jōcho; his work was intended for the Hōjō-ji. Much honoured in his lifetime, in 1022 he received an official religious appointment, known as 'Bridge of Law'. The canon he formulated was observed by successors, figures being sedate and gracious, finely detailed with rich drapes, with expressions suggestive of serenity and wisdom.

51 *Japanese art (Heian period) : Antira, one of the twelve guardians of Yakushi Nyorai. Painted relief on wood plaque. Nara, Kōfuku-ji.*

52 *Japanese art (Heian period) : Painted wood statue of prince Shōtoku, by the sculptors Enkai and Hata Chitei. AD* ***1069****. Nara, E-den of the Hōryū-ji.*

53 *Japanese art (Heian period) : Wood statue of Yakushi Nyorai. Late IX century AD. Nara, Gangō-ji.*

54 *Japanese art (Heian period): Gilded wood statue of Amida Nyorai, attributed to Jōchō. AD* **1053**. *Uji, Phoenix Hall of the Byōdō-in.*

55 *Japanese art (Heian period) : Figure of Bodhisattva Kokuzō. Tôkyô, National Museum.*

56 *Japanese art (Heian period) : Pilgrimage of Zenzai Doji to the fifty-five saints. Tôkyô, National Museum.*

51 Japanese art (Heian period): *Antira, one of the twelve guardians of Yakushi Nyorai*, painted relief on wood plaque. Nara, Kōfuku-ji.
The lively sense of movement expressed in this figure is of particular interest. Carved on a wood plaque, only traces of the ancient paint and gold leaf remain.

52 Japanese art (Heian period): *Painted wood statue of Prince Shōtoku*, by sculptors Enkai and Hata Chitei. AD 1069. Nara, E-den of the Hōryū-ji.
This statue of prince Shōtoku reflects the more relaxed style characteristic of the Fujiwara period.

53 Japanese art (Heian period): *Wood statue of Yakushi Nyorai*. Late IX century AD. Nara, Gangō-ji.
This statue is carved from a single block of wood, typical of the early Heian period.

54 Japanese art (Heian period): *Gilded wood statue of Amida Nyorai*, attributed to Jōchō. AD 1053. Uji, Phoenix Hall of the Byōdō-in.
This is an exceptionally fine example of Heian sculpture.

55 Japanese art (Heian period): *Figure of Bodhisattva Kokuzō*. Tôkyô, National Museum.
The lord of lovingkindness was a favourite subject for Heian painters. This figure is a fine example of the period.

56 Japanese art (Heian period): *Pilgrimage of Zenzai Doji to the fifty-five saints*. Tôkyô, National Museum.
A notable achievement, especially from the viewpoints of structure and composition.

57 Japanese art (Heian period): *Detail from the Tale of Prince Genji*. Early XII century AD. Tôkyô, Goto Museum.
Among the most original examples of the *yamato-e* style. Illustrations to stories were popular in the Heian period.

57 *Japanese art (Heian period) : Detail from the Tale of Prince Genji. Early XII century AD. Tôkyô, Goto Museum.*

Jōcho had a genius for depicting lifelike images that seemed on the point of breathing and moving. The work of his successors, by contrast, was often flabby and rather lifeless.

The cult of the deity often found expression, during the Heian period, in painting as well as in temple building and the making of sacred images. Painting, done on silk or on paper of various colours, was considered a morally improving occupation both for the artist and for the faithful who collected to admire the sacred subjects displayed in the temples.

Painting was carried out in strict accordance with binding rules and conventions. Subjects first had to be studied, after Chinese models, from black-and-white copies. There were two common types of representation: one was particularly complex, including all the officially recognized deities, painted in roundels or frames, the general effect being flat and of little variety. The other kind of painting was much more original and lively. Single images were depicted, with genuine freedom of expression. Among favourite themes in this style were the Heavenly Guardians, deities who were basically benign but fearsome enough in striking blows against enemies of the faith. Later, in the tenth and eleventh centuries, the standard of sacred painting was higher. Delicate and satisfying figures were produced, a typical masterpiece being the Bodhisattva Fugen, in Tôkyô National Museum. A certain degree of detachment, as compared with Chinese art, is evident. Even at its peak, the latter never quite achieved the intuitive sensitivity of Japanese painters in hand-

58 *Japanese art (Heian period) : Bodhisattva Fugen. Tôkyô, National Museum.*

59 *Japanese art (Heian period) : Detail of door in Phoenix Hall of the Byōdō-in at Uji.*

60 *Japanese art (Kamakura period) : North octagonal chamber of the Kōfuku-ji at Nara. AD 1208.*

61 *Japanese art (Kamakura period) : Pavilion of Relics in the Engaku-ji at Kamakura. AD 1279.*

58 Japanese art (Heian period): *Bodhisattva Fugen.* Tôkyô, National Museum.
Perhaps the most beautiful Japanese Buddhist painting. It is difficult to find fault either with the glowing colour or the seductive lines. Fujiwara period.

59 Japanese art (Heian period): *Detail of door in the Phoenix Hall of the Byōdō-in* at Uji.
The Phoenix Hall is splendidly decorated with a rich array of paintings depicting the *Paradise of Amida*.

60 Japanese art (Kamakura period): *North octagonal chamber of the Kōfuku-ji* at Nara. AD 1208.
In the great Kōfuku-ji complex at Nara, this north octagonal chamber is one of the oldest buildings.

61 Japanese art (Kamakura period): *Pavilion of Relics in the Engaku-ji* at Kamakura. AD 1279.
Classic example of 'Chinese' – style architecture, introduced into Japan during the Kamakura period. Associated with the rise of Zen Buddhism and only found in buildings of that denomination.

62 Japanese art (Kamakura period): *Great south gate of the Tōdai-ji* at Nara. Second half of XII century AD.
In the troubles that preceded the Kamakura period, the Tōdai-ji then standing was destroyed. A committee led by the priest Chōgen was responsible for rebuilding, in the Indian style called *tenjikuyō*.

63 Japanese art (Kamakura period): *Verses and figures on a fan panel.* Tôkyô, National Museum.
The painter made the figures from wood. These little blocks were moved about to create a number of different scenes, though the verses might thereby be hidden under the thick layers of colour.

62 *Japanese art (Kamakura period): Great south gate of the Tōdai-ji at Nara. Second half XII century AD.*

63 *Japanese art (Kamakura period): Verses and figures on a fan panel. Tôkyô, National Museum.*

ling sacred subjects. It is worth noting, in this connection, that it was in the year 999 that there was first mention of the term *yamato-e*, meaning Japanese as distinct from *kara-e* or Chinese-style painting.

In secular art, the disruptive trend was even more marked. Scrolls, of silk or paper, told a story, part text and part illustration. The fact that many of these works were by women accounts in some measure for their refinement and sentimental appeal. Subjects were sometimes make-believe and sometimes taken from everyday life. The pictures have charm, are delicately coloured and are occasionally detailed to the point of affectation. Among the best-known scroll paintings of this kind are the *Tale of Prince Genji* and the *Legends of Mt Shigi*. Furthermore, they are indicative of the standard of taste at the court in Kyôto – where feminine artistic achievement was held in high esteem by connoisseurs.

Towards the end of the twelfth century, the power of the Fujiwara family was undermined and then destroyed. A rebellion erupted and the outcome was military government. This centred on Kamakura, in the north-west, some 500 miles away from Kyôto. Political upheaval was accompanied by civil strife. Later there was the threat of Mongol invasion, but this was repelled. Austere living conditions led to a preoccupation with the after-life, and this religious frame of mind also influenced artistic expression. Contacts were resumed with China, and as a result there was a growing appreciation of the values of Sung and Yüan civilization. Among the imports was the part-religious, part-philosophical doctrine known as Zen (Ch'an, in China). The adherents of this way of life vehemently rejected the cult of relics and images. They followed the road of mysticism, grounded in the trials of everyday life. This new creed produced art forms that were stark and severe but full of tension and drama, compared with the more superficial Heian attitude to art as mere entertainment.

There was an interlude in architecture. A style – incorrectly called 'Indian' (*tenjikuyō* in Japanese) – was adopted for rebuilding the Tōdai-ji, under a special committee headed by the priest Chōgen. When activity was renewed, the style adopted was again reminiscent of the Chinese. The most important of the new temple buildings was the Engaku-ji, by Kamakura, dating from 1279. Zen standards endowed it with simplicity, linear grace and rational structure. Partly because of the prevailing mood, and partly as a result of the influence of Sung work from China, Japanese sculpture of the Kamakura period was notable for its realism. Salient examples of this trend are found in the works of the school of Unkei, a celebrated sculptor who trained his sons Kōben and Tankei to follow him.

Unkei was born at Nara, and thus had ample opportunity to study the naturalistic features of the temple sculptures of the Nara period four centuries earlier. But he added an indefinable quality of his own to produce marvels of portraiture. The statue that bears the name of Asagna the Indian sage is a speaking likeness of a Buddhist priest. This uncanny ability to

64 *Japanese art (Kamakura period): Portrait of Myōe Shonin attributed to Jōnin. AD 1230. Kyôto, Kōzan-ji.*

65 *Japanese art (Kamakura period) : Portrait of Minamoto-no-Yoritomo attributed to Fujiware Takanobu. Kyôto, Jingo-ji.*

Japanese art (Kamakura period) : (above) Detail from the Tale of Matsuraki njin. Yamaguchi, Bōfu Temmangu ; (below) Detail from the Life of the priest en. Tôkyô, National Museum.

64 Japanese art (Kamakura period): *Portrait of Myōe Shonin* attributed to Jōnin. AD 1230. Kyôto, Kōzan-ji. Ink and colour-wash, on paper. The linear interplay is fascinating, and has been attributed to Jōnin.

65 Japanese art (Kamakura period): *Portrait of Minamoto-no-Yoritomo* attributed to Fujiwara Takanobu. Kyôto, Jingo-ji.
Art of the Kamakura period has this enlivening streak of realism, achieving its greatest heights in the work of Fujiwara Takanobu. This famous portrait shows how well he deserved his reputation.

66 Japanese art (Kamakura period): (above) *Detail from the Tale of Matsuraki Tenjin.* Yamaguchi, Bōfu Temmangu; (below) *Detail from the Life of the priest Ippen.* Tôkyô, National Museum.
The tradition of richly-illustrated story scrolls continued in the Kamakura period. The *Tale of Matsuraki Tenjin* was a great favourite.

67 Japanese art (Kamakura period): *Figure of Mahatejas.* Tôkyô, Nezu Museum.
Lesser deities used to figure in the Buddha's company. This individual is a terrifying-looking monster.

68 Japanese art (Kamakura period): *Nachi Falls.* Early XIV century AD. Tôkyô, Nezu Museum.
This place had sacred associations. The work conveys a deeply reverent feeling even to the uninitiated viewer.

69 Japanese art (Kamakura period): *Kasuga Mandala.* *c.* AD 1300. Honolulu, Academy of Arts.
In the Kasuga shrine precinct stand the five protecting deities. Above, the sun's disc symbolizes the Vairocana Buddha, the Great Sun of Truth enlightening the world.

67 Japanese art (Kamakura period) : Figure of Mahc
Tôkyô, Nezu Museum.

68 *Japanese art (Kamakura period): Nachi Falls. Early XIV century AD. Tôkyô, Nezu Museum.*

69. *Japanese art (Kamakura period): Kasuga Mandala. c. AD 1300. Honolulu, Academy of Arts.*

seize on the essence of character and personal detail was inherited by his sons.
The Heavenly guardian Tentōki was just as vividly portrayed by his son Kōben; so too was the elderly Basu Sennin in a sculpture by another son Tankei. The same realistic treatment of the individual, rather than the general, was evident in the painting of the period, and there were many masterpieces of great dramatic strength. A superb example is the Minamoto-no-Yoritomo portrait, attributed to the painter Fujiwara Takanobu; in his work, Kamakura period art reached its pinnacle. The princely face, above the dark mass of his garment, heavy with a rhythm of broken lines, is serene and austere. Alongside this new style of painting, the earlier styles of both sacred and secular art continued to be developed, and there was some welcome experiment with new subjects and treatments. Compared with older forms, there is a clear gain in momentum and power. There is drama and terror in the frequently depicted scenes from the underworld and images of human victims of evil fate. Sometimes the Buddha was represented, coming down to earth to save the faithful. Scrolls telling a story were much in demand during the period, but the subjects were no longer those of the Heian period. In place of love stories, there were epics of war or adventure, conveyed with pace and passion and a genuine sense of excitement. Furthermore, painting in inks began at this time; as a medium, this had immense possibilities and was to be widely cultivated in succeeding ages. Production of art works in the

70 *Japanese art (Kamakura period) : Wood statue of patriarch Muchaku by the sculptor Unkei. AD 1208. Nara, Kōfuku-ji.*

71 *Japanese art (Kamakura period) : One of the eight companions of Fudō Miōō, work attributed to Unkei. Kongōbu-ji at Wakayama.*

72 *Japanese art (Kamakura period) : Demon lamp-stand, work by Kōben son of Unkei. AD 1215. Nara, Kōfuku-ji.*

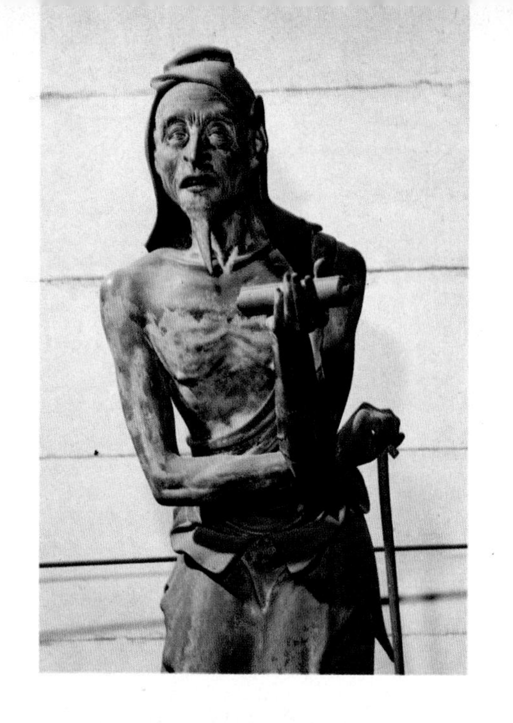

73 *Japanese art (Kamakura period) : Wood statue of monk Kūya, work by Kōshō. XIII century AD. Kyôto, Rokuharamitsu-ji*

74 *Japanese art (Kamakura period) : Wood statue of Basu Sennin, work by Tankei. XIII century AD. Kyôto, Renge-ō-in.*

75 *Japanese art (Kamakura period): Statue of Shō Kannon, work by Jōkei. AD **1226**. Kyôto, Kuramadera.*

70 Japanese art (Kamakura period): *Wood statue of patriarch Muchaku* by the sculptor Unkei. AD 1208. Nara, Kōfuku-ji.
Although not an exact and faithful likeness of a long-dead subject, this statue has realistic human features.

71 Japanese art (Kamakura period): *One of the eight companions of Fudō Miōō*, work attributed to Unkei. Kongōbu-ji at Wakayama.
The wealth of decorative detail in this painted wooden statue is unusual in work of the Kamakura period, which tended towards naturalism.

72 Japanese art (Kamakura period): *Demon lamp-stand*, work by Kōben son of Unkei. AD 1215. Nara, Kōfuku-ji.
This work by one of Unkei's sons, shows that he inherited his father's talent for strength and accuracy of detail.

73–4 Japanese art (Kamakura period): *Wood statue of monk Kūya*, work by Kōshō and *Wood statue of Basu Sennin*, work by Tankei (details). XIII century AD. Kyôtô, Rokuharamitsu-ji and Renge-ō-in.
These details from two statues show the high quality of sculpture of the Kamakura period.

75 Japanese art (Kamakura period): *Statue of Shō-Kannon*, work by Jōkei. AD 1226. Kyôto, Kurama-dera.
Attributes of the goddess of mercy, here represented, were a lotus flower and Amida crown.

76 Japanese art (Kamakura period): *'Great Buddha' of Kamakura*.
This statue dates from the year AD 1252. Variously ascribed by tradition to Ono Gorōraemon or Tanji Hisatomo. In 1452 the building that housed it was destroyed and since then it has remained in the open.

76 *Japanese art (Kamakura period) : 'Great Buddha' of Kamakura.*

Kamakura age was in fact as diversified as it had been in the preceding Heian period. Rich treatment continued to be given to ceramics, often on the Chinese model of lacquer set with precious metals. The motif of sword and dagger was frequently depicted, echoing the warrior values of the Kamakura shoguns.
In 1333 a military commander of noble blood, Ashikaga Takauji, overthrew the Kamakura dynasty and became shogun. The new government centred on Kyôto, in the Muromachi district. For over two centuries, the Ashikaga family held absolute power in Japan. In many respects, their civilization differed from the previous period. Contacts with China were deliberately fostered and Japan benefited from many aspects of Yüan and Ming culture. Although the government was a form of military despotism, there was peace and prosperity so that art and culture, under official encouragement, continued on a comparatively steady course. Zen Buddhism, which had already made a popular impact, was once more an active influence under the Ashikaga shoguns. Whereas under the Kamakura it had been regarded in some circles with suspicion, now, in the Muromachi period it found far wider acceptance. Zen ideals and rulings were translated into terms of everyday life. Zen priests were custodians of a remarkable moral system; their culture originated in India and had reached Japan through the intermediary of China, where it was appreciably enriched. Increasingly frequent contacts with the Chinese mainland assured the steady spiritual development of Japanese Zen.

Traditional Buddhism still attracted many believers, but no significant advance had been made since the Kamakura period. As a result, the arts most closely connected with it, especially sculpture, declined. The Zen code of ethics demanded no comparable external expression of the godhead. Painting of traditional Buddhist subjects were equally sterile, but painting in inks became increasingly popular, the technique being similar to that of Sung artists in China – in monochrome or light colour wash. For scroll painting, a special 'Indian' ink was employed, known in Japanese as *sumi*; from this was derived a local name for monochrome painting, *suiboku* (lit. 'painting done with water and *sumi*'). Indebted to Chinese models, the masters of Zen excelled in this field. Josetsu and his pupil, the monk Shūbun, were followed by Sesshū (1421–1507), acknowledged as the leading exponent of Japanese ink-painting. His landscapes are impressively varied in style but always show the highest degree of technical skill. After Sesshū came Kanō Masanobu and his son Motonobu. They originated the Kanō school which, with court patronage, produced a flourishing string of artists in the succeeding centuries. Early Kanō work used colour, not traditionally, but in the style of the Chinese school.

Another leading exponent of Japanese monochrome painting was the Buddhist monk Kenkō Shōkei (1478–1518), also known as Kei Shōki. The second name means secretary, describing his work in the Kenchō-ji, one of the five Zen monasteries at Kamakura. In the national tradition started by Shūbun, his ink land-

78 *Japanese art (Muromachi period): Winter landscape. Hanging scroll attributed to Sesshū. XV century AD. Tôkyô National Museum.*

77 *Japanese art (Muromachi period): Landscape attributed to Shūbun; ink and light colour-wash, on paper. XV century AD. Tôkyô, Nezu Museum.*

77 Japanese art (Muromachi period): *Landscape* attributed to Shūbun; ink and light colour-wash, on paper. XV century AD. Tôkyô, Nezu Museum.
In Japan during this period, Chinese civilization was a main source of influence – not for the first time. Monochrome painting followed the lead of Sung masters and its progress depended on that of Zen Buddhism as a Japanese pattern of life. The painters were frequently monks who came back from journeys to China bringing valuable art-works with them.

78 Japanese art (Muromachi period): *Winter landscape*. Hanging scroll attributed to Sesshū. XV century AD. Tôkyô, National Museum.
Japanese monochrome found a leading exponent in Sesshū, a Buddhist monk. His themes were traditional Chinese but the treatment showed a sound grasp of composition and supremely confident linear and ink values. The work illustrated came from a series dedicated to the four seasons; only autumn and winter remain.

79 Japanese art (Muromachi period): *Landscape*. Hanging scroll by Kenkō Shōkei. Tôkyô, Nezu Museum.
Another great expert in monochrome painting. Kenkō Shōkei was a Buddhist monk, pseudonym Kei Shōki. This derived from his work as *Shōki* (or secretary) at one of the five Zen monasteries in Kamakura. An eye for living reality marks his achievement, seldom surpassed.

80 Japanese art (Muromachi period): *Under the maples at Takao*, detail from a screen by Kanō Hideyori. Mid-XVI century AD. Tôkyô, National Museum.
This painting by Kanō Hideyori was something of a novelty at the time. But at a later date scenes from everyday life were much in demand.

79 *Japanese art (Muromachi period) : Landscape. Hang scroll by Kenko Shōkei. Tôkyô, Nezu Museum.*

scapes owed a good deal to the marvellous stylistic example set by Chinese masters. At the same time, he worked with an eye to the living reality of the scene selected. This inspiration from nature is a key to the rare quality of Shōkei's art.

Traditional *yamato-e* painting in brilliant colour appeared to be losing ground, though it was admirably represented by the Tosa school, founded in the closing years of the fifteenth century.

Muromachi architecture covered a mixture of styles, partially Chinese and partially derived from traditional Japanese models. No startling development occurred but many Zen temples of the period were soundly and tastefully constructed. Among notable private dwellings, subsequently given over to monastic use, were the Kinkakuji or Golden Pavilion (burned down in 1950 but rebuilt on the original plan) and the Ginkakuji or Silver Pavilion at Kyôto. The Golden Pavilion was named after its third storey, then as now, constructed entirely of gilt. Similar treatment was envisaged for the Silver Pavilion but the project did not materialize and only the name is left to record it.

The characteristically Japanese blend of elegance and good taste is seen in the Zen gardens of the period. Japan has a real genius for creating beauty on a miniature scale, many such works of art being masterpieces of grace and harmony. In Japanese art, the spectator is never overpowered by grandiose effects but seduced by the kind of charm and intimacy found in a floral arrangement or a combination of rocks, sand and foliage in a typical Zen garden. The sim-

Japanese art (Muromachi period): Under the maples at ...akao, detail from a screen by Kanō Hideyori. Mid-XVI ...ntury AD. Tôkyô, National Museum.

81 *Japanese art (Muromachi period) : Ginkakuji or Silver Pavilion of the Jishō-ji at Kyôto. XV century AD.*

82 *Japanese art (Muromachi period) : Kinkakuji or Golden Pavilion of the Rokuon-ji at Kyôto. XV century AD.*

81 Japanese art (Muromachi period): *Ginkakuji or Silver Pavilion of the Jishō-ji* at Kyôto. XV century AD.
A private residence in the luxury class; later converted for use as a monastery. The linear grace of the building speaks for itself.

82 Japanese art (Muromachi period): *Kinkakuji or Golden Pavilion of the Rokuon-ji* at Kyôto. XV century AD.
Like the Silver pavilion, a memorable tribute to Muromachi architecture. Burned down by fire in 1950, it was then faithfully rebuilt. The name is derived from the precious-metal finish given to the entire third storey.

83 Japanese art (Muromachi period): *Garden of the Daisen-in.* Kyôto.
The garden of the Daisen-in at Kyôto represents, in miniature, a vast natural landscape, with symbolic allusions. The rocks and trees in the background stand for distant mountains. Through them courses a river (the sand) which is crossed by a bridge (the flat rock). The whole composition is designed to scale and each feature fulfils a specific purpose.

84 Japanese art (Momoyama period): *Hiunkaku of the Nishi Hongan-ji* at Kyôto. XVII century AD.
The Hiunkaku of the Nishi Hongan-ji follows on from mainstream Muromachi architecture, exemplified in the Golden and Silver Pavilions. But there is more complexity and detail, characterizing the new Momoyama period.

83 *Japanese art (Muromachi period) : Garden of the Daisen-in. Kyôto.*

84 *Japanese art (Momoyama period) : Hiunkaku of the Nishi Hongan-ji at Kyôto. XVII century AD.*

plicity of these gardens is misleading, for they are full of rich and meaningful detail, very much in line with the painting of the age and perfectly reflecting the Japanese love of order and natural beauty. This same sensitivity and refinement of taste was echoed in other aspects of private and public life. Within the home, for example, there was the *tokonoma*, or point of display for an art work or special flower arrangement. Another was the *chaseki*, or room set aside for the tea ceremony. A Zen introduction, the tea ceremony was practised by the affluent upper classes and was synonymous with gracious living. The ceremony provided an opportunity for appreciating delicacies beautifully served and for stimulating conversation in pleasant surroundings. The tea ceremony called for appropriate tableware. Though strongly influenced by Chinese models, Japanese tea pottery nevertheless preserved individual features, inventive both in shape and decoration, most of it being stoneware but in some instances porcelain.

The closing years of the Muromachi period were darkened by the complete breakdown of law and order, as the ambitious nobility attempted to throw off the yoke of government. Consequently the country was divided into many separate pockets of power, and this predictably led to continuous and disruptive civil strife.

The task of pacification was undertaken, and successfully achieved, by two military commanders, Nobunaga and Hideyoshi, whose rise to power coincided with the Momoyama period. Although of fairly short

85 *Japanese art (Momoyama period-Edo period) : Shino ceramic bowl. Tôkyô, National Museum.*

86 *Japanese art (Momoyama period) : Oribe ceramic box. Tôkyô, Coll. priv.*

87 *Japanese art (Momoyama period): Pine-trees and plants, screen panel attributed to Hasegawa Tōhaku. Kyôto, Chishaku monastery.*

88 *Japanese art (Momoyama period) : Pine-trees, screen panel by Hasegawa Tōhaku. Tôkyô, National Museum.*

89 *Japanese art (Edo period) : Ho-tei at the river, painting by Kanō Tan-yū. Tôkyô, National Museum.*

90 *Japanese art (Edo period) : The mirror-seller, hanging scroll by Reizei Tamechika. Tôkyô, National Museum.*

85 Japanese art (Momoyama period – Edo period): *Shino ceramic bowl*. Tôkyô, National Museum.
Among the *Shino*-type ceramics, one group was called *Nezumi-shino*. This is distinguished by a greyish glaze.

86 Japanese art (Momoyama period): *Oribe ceramic box*. Tôkyô, Coll. priv.
Among the various types of ceramics, there are notable specimens known as *Oribe*, after the name of a celebrated tea-master, Furuta Oribe.

87 Japanese art (Momoyama period): *Pine-trees and plants*, screen panel attributed to Hasegawa Tōhaku. Kyôto, Chishaku Monastery.
A charming picture of plants growing under a pine-tree.

88 Japanese art (Momoyama period): *Pine-trees*, screen panel by Hasegawa Tōhaku. Tôkyô, National Museum.
Hasegawa Tōhaku excelled in a typically Chinese branch of art, namely monochrome ink painting.

91

89 Japanese art (Edo period): *Ho-tei at the river*, painting by Kanō Tan-yū. Tôkyô, National Museum.
Kanō Tan-yū was Takanobu's son. He later became painter by appointment to the shogun.

90 Japanese art (Edo period): *The mirror seller*, hanging scroll by Reizei Tamechika. Tôkyô, National Museum.
Reizei Tamechika won his reputation by restoring the 'Japanese style' of the days of Heian. The scroll concerns the merchant Sadamoto, who bought a mirror from a lady in distressed circumstances and then returned it.

91 Japanese art (Momoyama period): *Snow on cedars and cryptomerias*, Kanō school screen. XVII century AD. Washington, Freer Gallery of Art.
The boom in the decorative arts during the Momoyama period called for changes of style to meet popular demand, including painted doors, windows and screens. Black-and-white soon gave way to gorgeous colour.

duration (1573–1614) and in some ways to be regarded as a transitional period, it was of considerable social and cultural significance, for it represented a decisive reaction against earlier fashions. Its output was rich and the trends it initiated anticipated the broad artistic panorama of the Edo period which followed. Under military government the country gained a much-needed breathing space and enjoyed economic prosperity. The invasion of Korea in 1592, though it did not lead to permanent occupation, once again exposed Japan to the civilizing influence of that ancient land. For the first time there was a leisured and monied upper class – noblemen and landowners who demanded luxuries of all kinds. Art was subservient to their needs. Architectural taste and restraint went by the board. New buildings were lavish and ornate, decorated and often lacquered both inside and out. The Hiunkaku of the Nishi Hongan-ji, at Kyôto, is a typical example. Although in its overall conception it harks back to the Muromachi period and its masterpieces (the Golden and Silver pavilions), the component parts are much more varied and richly detailed. Among characteristic features of the Momoyama period are its dormers under pointed eaves, frequently seen on other palaces of the time, commissioned by high-ranking government officials and military commanders. The prolific use of gold and other precious metals symbolized the artistic standards of Momoyama society. This lavish display stimulated activity in the minor arts. Luxury articles were produced in large quantity and objects such as lacquered and multi-

92 *Japanese art (Edo period) : Irises, screen panel by Ōg*
Kōrin. Tôkyô, Nezu Museum.

92 Japanese art (Edo period): *Irises*, screen panel by Ōgata Kōrin. Tôkyô, Nezu Museum.
Ōgata Kōrin was the best-known follower of the school of Sōtatsu – always striving to express ideal beauty.

93 Japanese art (Edo period): *Figure of actor*, hanging scroll. Tôkyô, Nezu Museum.
The rising middle-class required rather impersonal, easily comprehended paintings.

94 Japanese art (Edo period): *Dawn at Uji*, by Aoki Mokubei. Tôkyô, Ministry of Education property.
Aoki Mokubei's landscapes are highly personal in style.

95 Japanese art (Edo period): *Hogai landscape*, of the Kanō school. Washington, Freer Gallery of Art.
Despite political isolation, Western influence filtered through to Japan during the eighteenth century. Painters, by and large, continued to treat typically Japanese themes.

96 Japanese art (Edo period): *Couple on veranda*, Suzuki Harunobu print. 1766 or 1767. Tôkyô, National Museum.
These figures are lithe and lovely. The secret lies in maintaining the linear flow.

97 Japanese art (Edo period): *Female figures* by Torii Kiyonaga. Tôkyô, Coll. Watanabe.
Torii Kiyonaga earned his reputation by portraying actors and a great variety of female figures.

98 Japanese art (Edo period): *Kambara*, from the series 'Fifty-three views along the Tōkaidō road' by Andō Hiroshige. Tôkyô, National Museum.
Andō Hiroshige made his name as a landscape painter. His winter scenes are especially successful.

93 *Japanese art (Edo period): Figure of actor, hanging scroll. Tôkyô, Nezu Museum.*

94 *Japanese art (Edo period) : Dawn at Uji, by Aoki Mokubei. Tôkyô, Ministry of Education property.*

95 *Japanese art (Edo period) : Hogai landscape, of the Kanō school. Washington, Freer Gallery of Art.*

96 *Japanese art (Edo period) : Couple on veranda, Suzuki Harunobu print.* ***1766*** *or* ***1767****. Tôkyô, National Museum.*

97 *Japanese art (Edo period) : Female figures by Torii Kiyonaga. Tôkyô, Coll. Watanabe.*

98 *Japanese art (Edo period) : Kambara, in the series 'Fifty-three views on the Tōkaidō road' by Andō Hiroshige. Tôkyô, National Museum.*

coloured toilet cases, and Korean-type ceramics, were highly valued. Painting was attuned to the prevailing mood and gold and silver were freely mingled with other colours. Typical of the Momoyama period were large painted screens for private residences. The screen-painters Eitoku, Sanraku and Sansetsu belonged to the famous Kanō 'family', and their compositions alternated the *yamato-e* style with *suiboku* or *sumi-e* (ink painting). Rival painters such as Yushō and Tōhaku worked in monochrome and modelled themselves on Chinese artists of the Ch'an sect like Mu Chi and Liang K'ai.
The seventeenth century ushered in the final phase of Japan's history, prior to modern times. The early part of the Edo period was dominated by the outstanding figure of Tokugawa Ieyasu, appointed shogun in 1603. He inaugurated new-style government, based on the policies of absolutism and containment. Under Ieyasu and his successors Japan was virtually isolated, especially from Western contacts, for some 250 years. The nobility were given enough latitude to ensure stable government and the new economic pattern encouraged the participation in national life of the lower classes – craftsmen and tradespeople. It was they who helped to influence subsequent development in the arts. Formerly, art had served the needs only of the privileged classes. Now there was popular taste to be considered as well. With a rich, well-grounded tradition behind it, painting was well equipped to branch out and experiment, and to meet the demand of the new market. *Yamato-e* painting, influenced by the

ostentatious Momoyama period and now with the addition of so-called *suiboku* (sweeping brush-strokes applying the ink to the silk), was the basis of the style of the remarkable Sōtatsu. But the best-known artist of this school was Ogata Kōrin (1658–1716). From his youth accustomed to fine surroundings, well educated, he modelled his work on that of Sōtatsu and the many paintings of the Momoyama period. He tried to paint ideal beauty, treating nature in an abstract rather than realistic manner, with extreme refinement and ingenuity. This painter, together with Kōetsu and the potter Kenzan, created the decorative school, full of colour and elegant floral devices. Their style still influences ceramic ware to the present time.

At the beginning of the Edo period, Miyamoto Masushi continued to paint in the *suiboku* manner, while the traditionalist Kanō school produced such masters as Tan-yū and his brother Naonobu. A new school, rooted in popular taste, was called *ukiyo-e* (figure painting), and depicted the customs and events of everyday life, treated in a straightforward and natural manner. Popular craving for art during the second half of the seventeenth century was in some measure satisfied by the introduction of *xylography*, or wood-block printing, invented by Moronobu (1618–94). His technique was subsequently improved by Harunobu (1725–70), a very celebrated artist, widely acclaimed during his lifetime. His colour prints, called *nishiki-e*, showed charming young women and tender love scenes.

Another painter in the style, Tōshūsai Sharaku, was

probably a theatre player of some distinction, though little is known of his life. His portraits of actors from the three main Kabuki theatres of Edo are singularly powerful and impressive. He painted only during a brief spell – over the ten months between May 1794 and February 1795. The painter Maruyama Ōkyo was a keen observer of nature and the human anatomy. It was he who inaugurated the *shijō* school ('Western painting'), active in Japan until recent years.
Among leading lights of the school of poet-painters, rather like the Chinese scholar-painters, reacting against the realistic approach, were Ike-no-Taiga and Yosa Buson.
The rather mixed group of *kan-ga* painters comprised scholars who saw painting purely as a leisure activity. They painted as they pleased, without seeking critical acclaim or adhering to scholastic rules. Aoki Mokubei (1767–1833) was among their number, noted for his individualism. Andō Hiroshige (1797–1858) was best known as a landscape painter: he in fact published a series of fifty-three views, drawn from the country-side along the road from Edo to Kyôto. His scenes share an appealing dreamlike quality, and the winter settings are especially noteworthy for their subtle effects of mist and wind.
There is a Japanese proverb, 'Don't talk of marvels until you've seen Nikkō!' The Tōshūgū (temple) erected in this city is one of the wonders of Japanese architecture and the decorative arts. Building com-plexes of the kind were echoed in other parts, during the Edo period. For the seventeenth and eighteenth

99 *Japanese art (Edo period) : The actor Bondō Mitsugorō in the role of Ishi-i Gensō, Tōshūsai Sharaku print. Tôkyô, National Museum.*

100 *Japanese art (Edo period) : Mt Fuji across the water, Katsushika Hokusai print. Tôkyô, National Museum.*

101 *Japanese art (Edo period) : Katsura Palace interior. XVII century AD.*

102 *Japanese art (Edo period): Katsura Palace interior. XVII century AD.*

99 Japanese art (Edo period): *The actor Bondō Mitsugorō in the role of Ishi-i Gensō*, Tōshūsai Sharaku print. Tôkyô, National Museum.
Very little is known about this actor-painter. Among his favourite subjects were the leading Kabuki theatre players of the time.

100 Japanese art (Edo period): *Mt Fuji across the water*, Katsushika Hokusai print. Tôkyô, National Museum.
This landscape is from the series, 'Thirty-six views of Mt Fuji'. The gigantic wave is typical of his mannered style.

101–2 Japanese art (Edo period): *Katsura Palace interiors*. XVII century AD.
The Imperial Prince Tomohito's country residence in former days, the interiors are noted for uncluttered elegance.

103 Japanese art (Edo period): *Katsura Palace buildings*. XVII century AD.
There are some notable out-buildings in the grounds of Katsura Palace. The pavilions harmonize well with the gardens.

104 Japanese art (Edo period): *Kutani porcelain dish*. Tôkyô, National Museum.
Kutani in Kaga province produced some of Japan's finest ceramics in the seventeenth century AD. Some authorities draw a comparison between the rich colour and design, and the decorative arts under the Momoyama.

105 Japanese art (Edo period): *Mt Yoshino vase*, by Ninsei. Tôkyô, Seikado Foundation.
The potter Ninsei was a maker of collector's pieces. This beautifully refined multi-coloured vase is one of his best known and most successful works.

103 *Japanese art (Edo period) : Katsura Palace buildings. XVII century AD.*

104 *Japanese art (Edo period): Kutani porcelain dish. Tôkyô, National Museum.*

105 *Japanese art (Edo period): Mt Yoshino vase, by Ninsei. Tôkyô, Seikado Foundation.*

centuries brought Japan prosperity, prerequisites for the construction of such imposing monuments. The style (almost Baroque) may seem elaborate to a fault; at the same time it must be admitted that the mass of gilt and lacquer is very impressive. Besides, delightful examples of contemporary buildings in simpler style can be found. In its garden setting, the Katsura summer palace – once of the Imperial prince Tomohito – is outstanding of its kind. The tea-house there deserves special mention, with its white paths and well-kept hedges. But it is to Nikkō that the mind returns. Here the carved gateways and interiors of the Tōshūgū show lacquer-work of the Edo period at its most superb.

The Edo period also saw a proliferation of the minor arts, and its products were highly prized in the West, so that they are nowadays found all over the civilized world. They too reveal those innate Japanese characteristics of good sense, grace and elegance, the touch of poetry which lights on what is small and fragile and transforms it into something rare and precious. This quiet beauty can be found in a spray of flowering cherry, or in the jewelled pin that sets off a *geisha* girl's hair.

TIME SCALE

KOREA

Period of the Three Kingdoms:	from the first century BC to the seventh century AD (Koguryō, Paekche, Silla)
Great Silla Kingdom:	from AD 668 to 918
Koryo period:	from AD 918 to 1392
Yi period:	from AD 1392 to 1910

JAPAN

Jōmon, Yayoi, Kofun periods:	from date unknown to AD 55
Asuka period:	from AD 552 to 645
Nara period:	from AD 645 to 794
Heian period:	from AD 794 to 1185
Kamakura period:	from AD 1185 to 1333
Muromachi period:	from AD 1333 to 1573
Momoyama period:	from AD 1573 to 1614
Edo period:	from AD 1614 to 1868
Modern period:	from AD 1868 to date.

BIBLIOGRAPHY

Korean art

H. B. CHAPIN, Palaces in Seoul, Transactions of the Korea Branch of the Royal Asiatic Society, XXXII, **1951***, pp.* **3–46**
G. GOMPERTZ, Korean Pottery and Porcelain of the Yi Period, New York, **1968**
G. GOMPERTZ, Koryo Inlaid Celadon Ware, Transactions of the Oriental Ceramic Society, XXVIII, **1953–4***, pp.* **37–50**
A. JANATA, Korean Painting, New York, **1964**

Japanese art

W. ALEX, Japanese Architecture, New York, **1963**
L. FREDERIC, Japan : Art and Civilization, New York, **1970**
J. HARADA, The Lesson of Japanese Architecture, 2nd edition, London **1954**
S. JENYNS, Japanese Porcelain, New York, **1965**
S. JENYNS, Japanese Pottery, New York, **1969**
J. E. KIDDER, Japanese Temples, New York, **1967**
R. A. MILLER, Japanese Ceramics, New York
W. S. MORTON, Japan : Its History and Culture, New York, **1970**
G. B. SANSON, Japan. A Short Cultural History, London **1946**
K. TODA, Japanese Painting, A Brief History, New York, **1965**
K. TODA, Japanese Scroll Painting, New York, **1969**

INDEX OF ILLUSTRATIONS